Building My Empire

PLANNER

THIS BOOK BELONGS TO

_____

MONTHLY BUSINESS PLAN

January	February	March

April	May	June

July	August	September

October	November	December

QUARTERLY BUSINESS PLAN

QUARTER ONE

QUARTER TWO

QUARTER THREE

QUARTER FOUR

MONTH

_____

MONTHLY BUSINESS GOALS

MONTH:

NEW CUSTOMERS:

CURRENT RANK:

VOLUME GOAL:

GOAL RANK:

COMMISSIONS:

NEW REPS:

Action Steps

To-Do

New Ideas

Promotions + Giveaways

MONTH:

THIS MONTHS GOALS

FRIENDS & FAMILY

. . . .

. . . .

. . . .

PERSONAL DEVELOPMENT

. . . .

. . . .

. . . .

SPIRITUALITY

. . . .

. . . .

. . . .

FINANCES

. . . .

. . . .

. . . .

CAREER

. . . .

. . . .

. . . .

RELATIONSHIP

. . . .

. . . .

. . . .

FUN & RECREATION

. . . .

. . . .

. . . .

GIVING & CONTRIBUTION

. . . .

. . . .

. . . .

ENVIRONMENT

. . . .

. . . .

. . . .

HEALTH & FITNESS

. . . .

. . . .

. . . .

Monday	*Tuesday*	*Wednesday*	*Thursday*

THIS MONTHS TOP 5 GOALS

☐ 1. _____

☐ 2. _____

☐ 3. _____

☐ 4. _____

☐ 5. _____

Friday	*Saturday*	*Sunday*

ACTIONS TO TAKE

☐ ....
☐ ....
☐ ....
☐ ....
☐ ....
☐ ....

NOTES

....
....
....
....
....
....
....
....
....
....
....
....
....

WHAT POSITIVE HABITS AND RITUALS DO I WANT TO CULTIVATE THIS MONTH?

☐ 1. _____
☐ 2. _____
☐ 3. _____
☐ 4. _____
☐ 5. _____

Weekly Plan & Goals

Dates / / - / /

1 ....
2 ....
3 ....
4 ....
5 ....

MONDAY

TUESDAY

WEDNESDAY

THURSDAY

FRIDAY

WEEKEND

TO-DO'S

home

- ☐
- ☐
- ☐
- ☐
- ☐
- ☐

work

- ☐
- ☐
- ☐
- ☐
- ☐
- ☐

GOALS GOAL // ACTUAL

New Customers
Commissions
New Team Members
Social Media Posts
Calls
Orders
New FB Friends
IG Following
Follow-Ups

Monday

Date   /   /

TODAYS TOP GOALS

1 ....
2 ....
3 ....

AFFIRMATIONS & GRATITUDE

TODAYS SCHEDULE

DAILY HABITS

SOCIAL MEDIA PLANNER

AM

12

PM

NOTES // IDEAS

TO-DO

Tuesday

Date   /   /

1 ....
2 ....
3 ....

AFFIRMATIONS & GRATITUDE

TODAYS SCHEDULE

DAILY HABITS

SOCIAL MEDIA PLANNER

AM

12

PM

NOTES//IDEAS

TO-DO

Wednesday

Date / /

TODAYS TOP GOALS

1 ....
2 ....
3 ....

AFFIRMATIONS & GRATITUDE

TODAYS SCHEDULE

DAILY HABITS

SOCIAL MEDIA PLANNER

AM

12

PM

NOTES // IDEAS

TO-DO

Thursday

Date   /   /

TODAYS TOP GOALS

1 ....
2 ....
3 ....

AFFIRMATIONS & GRATITUDE

TODAYS SCHEDULE

DAILY HABITS

SOCIAL MEDIA PLANNER

AM

12

PM

NOTES // IDEAS

TO-DO

Friday

Date / /

TODAYS TOP GOALS

1 ....
2 ....
3 ....

AFFIRMATIONS & GRATITUDE

TODAYS SCHEDULE

DAILY HABITS

SOCIAL MEDIA PLANNER

AM

12

PM

TO-DO

NOTES // IDEAS

Saturday

Date / /

AFFIRMATIONS & GRATITUDE

TODAYS SCHEDULE

DAILY HABITS

☐
☐
☐
☐
☐
☐

SOCIAL MEDIA PLANNER

AM

12

PM

TO-DO

☐
☐
☐
☐
☐
☐
☐
☐
☐

NOTES//IDEAS

Sunday

Date   /   /

TODAYS TOP GOALS

1 ....
2 ....
3 ....

AFFIRMATIONS & GRATITUDE

TODAYS SCHEDULE

DAILY HABITS

SOCIAL MEDIA PLANNER

AM

12

PM

TO-DO

NOTES // IDEAS

Weekly Plan & Goals

Dates / / - / /

1 ....
2 ....
3 ....
4 ....
5 ....

MONDAY

TUESDAY

WEDNESDAY

THURSDAY

FRIDAY

WEEKEND

TO-DO'S

home

☐
☐
☐
☐
☐
☐

work

☐
☐
☐
☐
☐

GOALS   GOAL//ACTUAL

New Customers
Commissions
New Team Members
Social Media Posts
Calls
Orders
New FB Friends
IG Following
Follow-Ups

Monday

Date   /   /

TODAYS TOP GOALS

1 ....

2 ....

3 ....

AFFIRMATIONS & GRATITUDE

TODAYS SCHEDULE

DAILY HABITS

☐
☐
☐
☐
☐
☐

SOCIAL MEDIA PLANNER

AM

12

PM

TO-DO

☐
☐
☐
☐
☐
☐
☐
☐
☐

NOTES//IDEAS

Tuesday

Date / /

TODAYS TOP GOALS

1 ....
2 ....
3 ....

AFFIRMATIONS & GRATITUDE

TODAYS SCHEDULE

DAILY HABITS

SOCIAL MEDIA PLANNER

AM

12

PM

NOTES // IDEAS

TO-DO

Wednesday

Date / /

TODAYS TOP GOALS

1 ....
2 ....
3 ....

AFFIRMATIONS & GRATITUDE

TODAYS SCHEDULE

DAILY HABITS

SOCIAL MEDIA PLANNER

AM

12

PM

NOTES // IDEAS

TO-DO

Thursday

Date   /   /

TODAYS TOP GOALS

1 ....
2 ....
3 ....

AFFIRMATIONS & GRATITUDE

TODAYS SCHEDULE

DAILY HABITS

SOCIAL MEDIA PLANNER

AM

12

PM

NOTES//IDEAS

TO-DO

Friday

Date   /   /

1 ....
2 ....
3 ....

AFFIRMATIONS & GRATITUDE

TODAYS SCHEDULE

DAILY HABITS

SOCIAL MEDIA PLANNER

AM

12

PM

NOTES // IDEAS

TO-DO

Saturday

Date   /   /

TODAYS TOP GOALS
1 ....
2 ....
3 ....

AFFIRMATIONS & GRATITUDE

TODAYS SCHEDULE

DAILY HABITS

SOCIAL MEDIA PLANNER

AM

12

PM

NOTES//IDEAS

TO-DO

Sunday

Date   /   /

TODAYS TOP GOALS

1 ....
2 ....
3 ....

AFFIRMATIONS & GRATITUDE

TODAYS SCHEDULE

DAILY HABITS

☐
☐
☐
☐
☐
☐

SOCIAL MEDIA PLANNER

AM

12

PM

NOTES//IDEAS

TO-DO

☐
☐
☐
☐
☐
☐
☐
☐
☐

Weekly Plan & Goals

Dates / / - / /

1 ....
2 ....
3 ....
4 ....
5 ....

MONDAY

TUESDAY

WEDNESDAY

THURSDAY

FRIDAY

WEEKEND

TO-DO'S

home

- [ ]
- [ ]
- [ ]
- [ ]
- [ ]
- [ ]

work

- [ ]
- [ ]
- [ ]
- [ ]
- [ ]
- [ ]

GOALS GOAL//ACTUAL

New Customers
Commissions
New Team Members
Social Media Posts
Calls
Orders
New FB Friends
IG Following
Follow-Ups

Monday

Date   /   /

TODAYS TOP GOALS

1 ....
2 ....
3 ....

AFFIRMATIONS & GRATITUDE

TODAYS SCHEDULE

DAILY HABITS

SOCIAL MEDIA PLANNER

AM

12

PM

TO-DO

NOTES // IDEAS

Tuesday

Date   /   /

1 ....
2 ....
3 ....

AFFIRMATIONS & GRATITUDE

TODAYS SCHEDULE

DAILY HABITS

SOCIAL MEDIA PLANNER

AM

12

PM

TO-DO

NOTES // IDEAS

Wednesday

1 ....
2 ....
3 ....

Date   /   /

AFFIRMATIONS & GRATITUDE

TODAYS SCHEDULE

DAILY HABITS

☐
☐
☐
☐
☐
☐

SOCIAL MEDIA PLANNER

AM

12

PM

NOTES // IDEAS

TO-DO

☐
☐
☐
☐
☐
☐
☐
☐
☐

Thursday

Date   /   /

1 ....

2 ....

3 ....

AFFIRMATIONS & GRATITUDE

TODAYS SCHEDULE

DAILY HABITS

SOCIAL MEDIA PLANNER

AM

12

PM

TO-DO

NOTES // IDEAS

Friday

Date   /   /

AFFIRMATIONS & GRATITUDE

TODAYS SCHEDULE

DAILY HABITS

SOCIAL MEDIA PLANNER

AM

12

PM

NOTES // IDEAS

TO-DO

Saturday

Date   /   /

1 . . . .
2 . . . .
3 . . . .

AFFIRMATIONS & GRATITUDE

TODAYS SCHEDULE

DAILY HABITS

SOCIAL MEDIA PLANNER

AM

12

PM

NOTES // IDEAS

TO-DO

Sunday

Date   /   /

AFFIRMATIONS & GRATITUDE

TODAYS SCHEDULE

DAILY HABITS

SOCIAL MEDIA PLANNER

AM

12

PM

TO-DO

NOTES//IDEAS

Weekly Plan & Goals

Dates / / - / /

1
2
3
4
5

MONDAY

TUESDAY

WEDNESDAY

THURSDAY

FRIDAY

WEEKEND

TO·DO'S

home

☐
☐
☐
☐
☐
☐

work

☐
☐
☐
☐
☐

GOALS
GOAL//ACTUAL

New Customers
Commissions
New Team Members
Social Media Posts
Calls
Orders
New FB Friends
IG Following
Follow-Ups

Monday

Date / /

TODAYS TOP GOALS

1 ....
2 ....
3 ....

AFFIRMATIONS & GRATITUDE

TODAYS SCHEDULE

DAILY HABITS

SOCIAL MEDIA PLANNER

AM

12

PM

TO-DO

NOTES // IDEAS

Tuesday

Date   /   /

TODAYS TOP GOALS

1 . . . .
2 . . . .
3 . . . .

AFFIRMATIONS & GRATITUDE

TODAYS SCHEDULE

DAILY HABITS

SOCIAL MEDIA PLANNER

AM

12

PM

TO-DO

NOTES//IDEAS

Wednesday

Date / /

TODAYS TOP GOALS

1 ....

2 ....

3 ....

AFFIRMATIONS & GRATITUDE

TODAYS SCHEDULE

DAILY HABITS

SOCIAL MEDIA PLANNER

AM

12

PM

NOTES//IDEAS

TO-DO

Thursday

Date   /   /

1 ....
2 ....
3 ....

AFFIRMATIONS & GRATITUDE

TODAYS SCHEDULE

DAILY HABITS

SOCIAL MEDIA PLANNER

AM

12

PM

NOTES // IDEAS

TO-DO

Friday

Date   /   /

1 ....
2 ....
3 ....

AFFIRMATIONS & GRATITUDE

TODAYS SCHEDULE

DAILY HABITS

- [ ]
- [ ]
- [ ]
- [ ]
- [ ]
- [ ]

SOCIAL MEDIA PLANNER

AM

12

PM

NOTES//IDEAS

TO-DO

- [ ]
- [ ]
- [ ]
- [ ]
- [ ]
- [ ]
- [ ]
- [ ]

Saturday

Date / /

1 ....
2 ....
3 ....

AFFIRMATIONS & GRATITUDE

TODAYS SCHEDULE

DAILY HABITS

SOCIAL MEDIA PLANNER

AM

12

PM

NOTES//IDEAS

TO-DO

Sunday

Date / /

TODAYS TOP GOALS

1 ....
2 ....
3 ....

AFFIRMATIONS & GRATITUDE

TODAYS SCHEDULE

DAILY HABITS

SOCIAL MEDIA PLANNER

AM

12

PM

NOTES//IDEAS

TO-DO

MONTH

MONTHLY BUSINESS GOALS

MONTH:

NEW CUSTOMERS:

CURRENT RANK:

VOLUME GOAL:

GOAL RANK:

COMMISSIONS:

NEW REPS:

Action Steps

To-Do

New Ideas

Promotions + Giveaways

MONTH:

THIS MONTHS GOALS

FRIENDS & FAMILY

. . . .
. . . .
. . . .

PERSONAL DEVELOPMENT

. . . .
. . . .
. . . .

SPIRITUALITY

. . . .
. . . .
. . . .

FINANCES

. . . .
. . . .
. . . .

CAREER

. . . .
. . . .
. . . .

RELATIONSHIP

. . . .
. . . .
. . . .

FUN & RECREATION

. . . .
. . . .
. . . .

GIVING & CONTRIBUTION

. . . .
. . . .
. . . .

ENVIRONMENT

. . . .
. . . .
. . . .

HEALTH & FITNESS

. . . .
. . . .
. . . .

Monday	*Tuesday*	*Wednesday*	*Thursday*

THIS MONTHS TOP 5 GOALS

☐ 1. _____

☐ 2. _____

☐ 3. _____

☐ 4. _____

☐ 5. _____

	Friday	*Saturday*	*Sunday*

ACTIONS TO TAKE

☐ ....
☐ ....
☐ ....
☐ ....
☐ ....
☐ ....

NOTES

....
....
....
....
....
....
....
....
....
....
....
....
....
....

WHAT POSITIVE HABITS AND RITUALS DO I WANT TO CULTIVATE THIS MONTH?

☐ 1. _____
☐ 2. _____
☐ 3. _____
☐ 4. _____
☐ 5. _____

Weekly Plan & Goals

Dates / / - / /

1 ....
2 ....
3 ....
4 ....
5 ....

MONDAY

TUESDAY

WEDNESDAY

THURSDAY

FRIDAY

WEEKEND

TO-DO'S

home

- ☐
- ☐
- ☐
- ☐
- ☐
- ☐

work

- ☐
- ☐
- ☐
- ☐
- ☐
- ☐

GOALS GOAL//ACTUAL

New Customers
Commissions
New Team Members
Social Media Posts
Calls
Orders
New FB Friends
IG Following
Follow-Ups

Monday

Date   /   /

1 ....
2 ....
3 ....

AFFIRMATIONS & GRATITUDE

TODAYS SCHEDULE

DAILY HABITS

☐
☐
☐
☐
☐
☐

SOCIAL MEDIA PLANNER

AM

12

PM

TO-DO

☐
☐
☐
☐
☐
☐
☐
☐
☐

NOTES // IDEAS

Tuesday

TODAYS TOP GOALS

1 ....
2 ....
3 ....

Date   /   /

AFFIRMATIONS & GRATITUDE

TODAYS SCHEDULE

DAILY HABITS

SOCIAL MEDIA PLANNER

AM

12

PM

TO-DO

NOTES//IDEAS

Wednesday

Date   /   /

1 ....
2 ....
3 ....

AFFIRMATIONS & GRATITUDE

TODAYS SCHEDULE

DAILY HABITS

☐
☐
☐
☐
☐
☐

SOCIAL MEDIA PLANNER

AM

12

PM

NOTES // IDEAS

TO-DO

☐
☐
☐
☐
☐
☐
☐
☐
☐

Thursday

Date   /   /

1 ....

2 ....

3 ....

AFFIRMATIONS & GRATITUDE

TODAYS SCHEDULE

DAILY HABITS

☐
☐
☐
☐
☐
☐

SOCIAL MEDIA PLANNER

AM

12

PM

NOTES//IDEAS

TO-DO

☐
☐
☐
☐
☐
☐
☐
☐

Friday

Date   /   /

TODAYS TOP GOALS

1 ....

2 ....

3 ....

AFFIRMATIONS & GRATITUDE

TODAYS SCHEDULE

DAILY HABITS

- [ ]
- [ ]
- [ ]
- [ ]
- [ ]
- [ ]

SOCIAL MEDIA PLANNER

AM

12

PM

TO-DO

- [ ]
- [ ]
- [ ]
- [ ]
- [ ]
- [ ]
- [ ]
- [ ]
- [ ]
- [ ]

NOTES // IDEAS

Saturday

Date / /

1 ....
2 ....
3 ....

AFFIRMATIONS & GRATITUDE

TODAYS SCHEDULE

DAILY HABITS

SOCIAL MEDIA PLANNER

AM

12

PM

TO-DO

NOTES // IDEAS

Sunday

Date / /

TODAYS TOP GOALS

1 ....
2 ....
3 ....

AFFIRMATIONS & GRATITUDE

TODAYS SCHEDULE

DAILY HABITS

- [ ]
- [ ]
- [ ]
- [ ]
- [ ]
- [ ]

SOCIAL MEDIA PLANNER

AM

12

PM

TO-DO

- [ ]
- [ ]
- [ ]
- [ ]
- [ ]
- [ ]
- [ ]
- [ ]
- [ ]

NOTES//IDEAS

Weekly Plan & Goals

Dates / / - / /

1 ....
2 ....
3 ....
4 ....
5 ....

MONDAY

TUESDAY

WEDNESDAY

THURSDAY

FRIDAY

WEEKEND

TO-DO'S

home

☐
☐
☐
☐
☐
☐

work

☐
☐
☐
☐
☐

GOALS   GOAL//ACTUAL

New Customers
Commissions
New Team Members
Social Media Posts
Calls
Orders
New FB Friends
IG Following
Follow-Ups

Monday

Date / /

TODAYS TOP GOALS

1 ....
2 ....
3 ....

AFFIRMATIONS & GRATITUDE

TODAYS SCHEDULE

DAILY HABITS

SOCIAL MEDIA PLANNER

AM

12

PM

TO-DO

NOTES // IDEAS

Tuesday

Date   /   /

AFFIRMATIONS & GRATITUDE

TODAYS SCHEDULE

DAILY HABITS

SOCIAL MEDIA PLANNER

AM

12

PM

TO-DO

NOTES//IDEAS

Wednesday

Date   /   /

1 ....
2 ....
3 ....

AFFIRMATIONS & GRATITUDE

TODAYS SCHEDULE

DAILY HABITS

SOCIAL MEDIA PLANNER

AM

12

PM

TO-DO

NOTES // IDEAS

Thursday

Date / /

1 ....
2 ....
3 ....

AFFIRMATIONS & GRATITUDE

TODAYS SCHEDULE

DAILY HABITS

- [ ]
- [ ]
- [ ]
- [ ]
- [ ]
- [ ]

SOCIAL MEDIA PLANNER

AM

12

PM

NOTES//IDEAS

TO-DO

- [ ]
- [ ]
- [ ]
- [ ]
- [ ]
- [ ]
- [ ]
- [ ]
- [ ]

Friday

Date / /

1 ....
2 ....
3 ....

AFFIRMATIONS & GRATITUDE

TODAYS SCHEDULE

DAILY HABITS

- [ ]
- [ ]
- [ ]
- [ ]
- [ ]
- [ ]

SOCIAL MEDIA PLANNER

AM

12

PM

TO-DO

- [ ]
- [ ]
- [ ]
- [ ]
- [ ]
- [ ]
- [ ]
- [ ]
- [ ]

NOTES // IDEAS

Saturday

Date   /   /

1 . . . .
2 . . . .
3 . . . .

AFFIRMATIONS & GRATITUDE

TODAYS SCHEDULE

DAILY HABITS

SOCIAL MEDIA PLANNER

AM

12

PM

NOTES//IDEAS

TO-DO

Sunday

Date / /

1 ....
2 ....
3 ....

AFFIRMATIONS & GRATITUDE

TODAYS SCHEDULE

DAILY HABITS

☐
☐
☐
☐
☐
☐

SOCIAL MEDIA PLANNER

AM

12

PM

NOTES // IDEAS

TO-DO

☐
☐
☐
☐
☐
☐
☐
☐

Weekly Plan & Goals

Dates / / - / /

1 ....
2 ....
3 ....
4 ....
5 ....

TO-DO'S

home
☐
☐
☐
☐
☐
☐

work
☐
☐
☐
☐
☐

| MONDAY |
| TUESDAY |
| WEDNESDAY |
| THURSDAY |
| FRIDAY |
| WEEKEND |

GOALS GOAL//ACTUAL

New Customers
Commissions
New Team Members
Social Media Posts
Calls
Orders
New FB Friends
IG Following
Follow-Ups

Monday

Date   /   /

TODAYS TOP GOALS

1 ....
2 ....
3 ....

AFFIRMATIONS & GRATITUDE

TODAYS SCHEDULE

DAILY HABITS

- ☐
- ☐
- ☐
- ☐
- ☐
- ☐

SOCIAL MEDIA PLANNER

AM

12

PM

NOTES // IDEAS

TO-DO

- ☐
- ☐
- ☐
- ☐
- ☐
- ☐
- ☐
- ☐
- ☐

Tuesday

Date   /   /

1 ....
2 ....
3 ....

AFFIRMATIONS & GRATITUDE

TODAYS SCHEDULE

DAILY HABITS

- [ ]
- [ ]
- [ ]
- [ ]
- [ ]
- [ ]

SOCIAL MEDIA PLANNER

AM

12

PM

TO-DO

- [ ]
- [ ]
- [ ]
- [ ]
- [ ]
- [ ]
- [ ]
- [ ]
- [ ]
- [ ]

NOTES // IDEAS

Wednesday

1 ....
2 ....
3 ....

Date   /   /

AFFIRMATIONS & GRATITUDE

TODAYS SCHEDULE

DAILY HABITS

SOCIAL MEDIA PLANNER

AM

12

PM

NOTES//IDEAS

TO-DO

Thursday

Date   /   /

1 ....
2 ....
3 ....

AFFIRMATIONS & GRATITUDE

TODAYS SCHEDULE

DAILY HABITS

☐
☐
☐
☐
☐
☐

SOCIAL MEDIA PLANNER

AM

12

PM

NOTES // IDEAS

TO-DO

☐
☐
☐
☐
☐
☐
☐
☐
☐
☐

Friday

Date   /   /

TODAYS TOP GOALS

1 ....
2 ....
3 ....

AFFIRMATIONS & GRATITUDE

TODAYS SCHEDULE

DAILY HABITS

SOCIAL MEDIA PLANNER

AM

12

PM

TO-DO

NOTES // IDEAS

Saturday

Date / /

TODAYS TOP GOALS

1 ....
2 ....
3 ....

AFFIRMATIONS & GRATITUDE

TODAYS SCHEDULE

DAILY HABITS

SOCIAL MEDIA PLANNER

AM

12

PM

TO-DO

NOTES // IDEAS

Sunday

Date   /   /

TODAYS TOP GOALS

1 ....
2 ....
3 ....

AFFIRMATIONS & GRATITUDE

TODAYS SCHEDULE

DAILY HABITS

SOCIAL MEDIA PLANNER

AM

12

PM

NOTES//IDEAS

TO-DO

Weekly Plan & Goals

Dates / / - / /

1 ....
2 ....
3 ....
4 ....
5 ....

MONDAY

TUESDAY

WEDNESDAY

THURSDAY

FRIDAY

WEEKEND

TO-DO'S

home

- ☐
- ☐
- ☐
- ☐
- ☐
- ☐

work

- ☐
- ☐
- ☐
- ☐
- ☐

GOALS GOAL//ACTUAL

New Customers

Commissions

New Team Members

Social Media Posts

Calls

Orders

New FB Friends

IG Following

Follow-Ups

....

....

....

....

Monday

Date / /

TODAYS TOP GOALS

1 ....
2 ....
3 ....

AFFIRMATIONS & GRATITUDE

TODAYS SCHEDULE

DAILY HABITS

SOCIAL MEDIA PLANNER

AM

12

PM

NOTES // IDEAS

TO-DO

Tuesday

Date   /   /

TODAYS TOP GOALS

1 ....

2 ....

3 ....

AFFIRMATIONS & GRATITUDE

TODAYS SCHEDULE

DAILY HABITS

SOCIAL MEDIA PLANNER

AM

12

PM

NOTES // IDEAS

TO-DO

Wednesday

Date   /   /

1 ....

2 ....

3 ....

AFFIRMATIONS & GRATITUDE

TODAYS SCHEDULE

DAILY HABITS

- [ ]
- [ ]
- [ ]
- [ ]
- [ ]
- [ ]

SOCIAL MEDIA PLANNER

AM

12

PM

NOTES // IDEAS

TO-DO

- [ ]
- [ ]
- [ ]
- [ ]
- [ ]
- [ ]
- [ ]
- [ ]

Thursday

Date   /   /

1 ....
2 ....
3 ....

AFFIRMATIONS & GRATITUDE

TODAYS SCHEDULE

DAILY HABITS

SOCIAL MEDIA PLANNER

AM

12

PM

NOTES // IDEAS

TO-DO

Friday

Date   /   /

1 . . . .
2 . . . .
3 . . . .

AFFIRMATIONS & GRATITUDE

TODAYS SCHEDULE

DAILY HABITS

SOCIAL MEDIA PLANNER

AM

12

PM

TO-DO

NOTES // IDEAS

Saturday

Date   /   /

TODAYS TOP GOALS

1 . . . .
2 . . . .
3 . . . .

AFFIRMATIONS & GRATITUDE

TODAYS SCHEDULE

DAILY HABITS

SOCIAL MEDIA PLANNER

AM

12

PM

NOTES//IDEAS

TO-DO

Sunday

Date / /

1 ....
2 ....
3 ....

AFFIRMATIONS & GRATITUDE

TODAYS SCHEDULE

DAILY HABITS

- [ ]
- [ ]
- [ ]
- [ ]
- [ ]
- [ ]

SOCIAL MEDIA PLANNER

AM

12

PM

TO-DO

- [ ]
- [ ]
- [ ]
- [ ]
- [ ]
- [ ]
- [ ]
- [ ]
- [ ]

NOTES // IDEAS

MONTH

_____

MONTHLY BUSINESS GOALS

MONTH:

NEW CUSTOMERS:

CURRENT RANK:

VOLUME GOAL:

GOAL RANK:

COMMISSIONS:

NEW REPS:

Action Steps

To-Do

New Ideas

Promotions + Giveaways

MONTH:

THIS MONTHS GOALS

FRIENDS & FAMILY

· ·

· ·

· ·

PERSONAL DEVELOPMENT

· ·

· ·

· ·

SPIRITUALITY

· ·

· ·

· ·

FINANCES

· ·

· ·

· ·

CAREER

· ·

· ·

· ·

RELATIONSHIP

· ·

· ·

· ·

FUN & RECREATION

· ·

· ·

· ·

GIVING & CONTRIBUTION

· ·

· ·

· ·

ENVIRONMENT

· ·

· ·

· ·

HEALTH & FITNESS

· ·

· ·

· ·

Monday	*Tuesday*	*Wednesday*	*Thursday*

THIS MONTHS TOP 5 GOALS

☐ 1. _____

☐ 2. _____

☐ 3. _____

☐ 4. _____

☐ 5. _____

Friday   *Saturday*   *Sunday*

ACTIONS TO TAKE

☐ ....
☐ ....
☐ ....
☐ ....
☐ ....
☐ ....

NOTES

....
....
....
....
....
....
....
....
....
....
....
....
....
....

WHAT POSITIVE HABITS AND RITUALS DO I WANT TO CULTIVATE THIS MONTH?

☐ 1. _____
☐ 2. _____
☐ 3. _____
☐ 4. _____
☐ 5. _____

Weekly Plan & Goals

Dates / / - / /

1 ....

2 ....

3 ....

4 ....

5 ....

MONDAY

TUESDAY

WEDNESDAY

THURSDAY

FRIDAY

WEEKEND

TO-DO'S

h o m e

- ☐
- ☐
- ☐
- ☐
- ☐
- ☐

w o r k

- ☐
- ☐
- ☐
- ☐
- ☐
- ☐

GOALS   GOAL//ACTUAL

New Customers

Commissions

New Team Members

Social Media Posts

Calls

Orders

New FB Friends

IG Following

Follow-Ups

Monday

Date   /   /

1 ....
2 ....
3 ....

AFFIRMATIONS & GRATITUDE

TODAYS SCHEDULE

DAILY HABITS

☐
☐
☐
☐
☐
☐

SOCIAL MEDIA PLANNER

AM

12

PM

TO-DO

☐
☐
☐
☐
☐
☐
☐
☐
☐

NOTES // IDEAS

Tuesday

Date   /   /

TODAYS TOP GOALS

1 ....
2 ....
3 ....

AFFIRMATIONS & GRATITUDE

TODAYS SCHEDULE

DAILY HABITS

- [ ]
- [ ]
- [ ]
- [ ]
- [ ]
- [ ]

SOCIAL MEDIA PLANNER

AM

12

PM

TO-DO

- [ ]
- [ ]
- [ ]
- [ ]
- [ ]
- [ ]
- [ ]
- [ ]
- [ ]

NOTES//IDEAS

Wednesday

Date   /   /

TODAYS TOP GOALS

1 ....
2 ....
3 ....

AFFIRMATIONS & GRATITUDE

TODAYS SCHEDULE

DAILY HABITS

- [ ]
- [ ]
- [ ]
- [ ]
- [ ]
- [ ]

SOCIAL MEDIA PLANNER

AM

12

PM

NOTES // IDEAS

TO-DO

- [ ]
- [ ]
- [ ]
- [ ]
- [ ]
- [ ]
- [ ]
- [ ]
- [ ]

Thursday

Date   /   /

1 ....
2 ....
3 ....

AFFIRMATIONS & GRATITUDE

TODAYS SCHEDULE

DAILY HABITS

SOCIAL MEDIA PLANNER

AM

12

PM

NOTES//IDEAS

TO-DO

Friday

Date   /   /

TODAYS TOP GOALS

1 ....
2 ....
3 ....

AFFIRMATIONS & GRATITUDE

TODAYS SCHEDULE

DAILY HABITS

SOCIAL MEDIA PLANNER

AM

12

PM

NOTES // IDEAS

TO-DO

Saturday

Date   /   /

TODAYS TOP GOALS

1 ....
2 ....
3 ....

AFFIRMATIONS & GRATITUDE

TODAYS SCHEDULE

DAILY HABITS

SOCIAL MEDIA PLANNER

AM

12

PM

NOTES//IDEAS

TO-DO

Sunday

Date   /   /

TODAYS TOP GOALS

1 ....
2 ....
3 ....

AFFIRMATIONS & GRATITUDE

TODAYS SCHEDULE

DAILY HABITS

- ☐
- ☐
- ☐
- ☐
- ☐
- ☐

SOCIAL MEDIA PLANNER

AM

12

PM

NOTES // IDEAS

TO-DO

- ☐
- ☐
- ☐
- ☐
- ☐
- ☐
- ☐
- ☐
- ☐

Weekly Plan & Goals

Dates / / - / /

1 ....
2 ....
3 ....
4 ....
5 ....

MONDAY

TUESDAY

WEDNESDAY

THURSDAY

FRIDAY

WEEKEND

TO-DO'S

home

- [ ]
- [ ]
- [ ]
- [ ]
- [ ]
- [ ]

work

- [ ]
- [ ]
- [ ]
- [ ]
- [ ]

GOALS   GOAL//ACTUAL

New Customers
Commissions
New Team Members
Social Media Posts
Calls
Orders
New FB Friends
IG Following
Follow-Ups

Monday

1 ....
2 ....
3 ....

Date   /   /

AFFIRMATIONS & GRATITUDE

TODAYS SCHEDULE

DAILY HABITS

☐
☐
☐
☐
☐
☐

SOCIAL MEDIA PLANNER

AM

12

PM

TO-DO

☐
☐
☐
☐
☐
☐
☐
☐
☐

NOTES // IDEAS

Tuesday

Date / /

TODAYS TOP GOALS

1 ....
2 ....
3 ....

AFFIRMATIONS & GRATITUDE

TODAYS SCHEDULE

DAILY HABITS

- ☐
- ☐
- ☐
- ☐
- ☐
- ☐

SOCIAL MEDIA PLANNER

AM

12

PM

NOTES//IDEAS

TO-DO

- ☐
- ☐
- ☐
- ☐
- ☐
- ☐
- ☐
- ☐
- ☐

Wednesday

Date   /   /

AFFIRMATIONS & GRATITUDE

TODAYS SCHEDULE

DAILY HABITS

SOCIAL MEDIA PLANNER

AM

12

PM

NOTES // IDEAS

TO-DO

Thursday

Date / /

1 ....
2 ....
3 ....

AFFIRMATIONS & GRATITUDE

TODAYS SCHEDULE

DAILY HABITS

SOCIAL MEDIA PLANNER

AM

12

PM

NOTES // IDEAS

TO-DO

Friday

Date / /

TODAYS TOP GOALS

1 ....

2 ....

3 ....

AFFIRMATIONS & GRATITUDE

TODAYS SCHEDULE

DAILY HABITS

- ☐
- ☐
- ☐
- ☐
- ☐
- ☐

SOCIAL MEDIA PLANNER

AM

12

PM

NOTES//IDEAS

TO-DO

- ☐
- ☐
- ☐
- ☐
- ☐
- ☐
- ☐
- ☐
- ☐
- ☐

Saturday

Date   /   /

1 ....

2 ....

3 ....

AFFIRMATIONS & GRATITUDE

TODAYS SCHEDULE

DAILY HABITS

SOCIAL MEDIA PLANNER

AM

12

PM

TO-DO

NOTES//IDEAS

Sunday

Date / /

TODAYS TOP GOALS

1 . . . .
2 . . . .
3 . . . .

AFFIRMATIONS & GRATITUDE

TODAYS SCHEDULE

DAILY HABITS

- [ ]
- [ ]
- [ ]
- [ ]
- [ ]
- [ ]

SOCIAL MEDIA PLANNER

AM

12

PM

NOTES // IDEAS

TO-DO

- [ ]
- [ ]
- [ ]
- [ ]
- [ ]
- [ ]
- [ ]
- [ ]
- [ ]

Weekly Plan & Goals

Dates   /   /   -   /   /

1 ....
2 ....
3 ....
4 ....
5 ....

MONDAY

TUESDAY

WEDNESDAY

THURSDAY

FRIDAY

WEEKEND

TO-DO'S

home

☐
☐
☐
☐
☐
☐

work

☐
☐
☐
☐
☐
☐

GOALS   GOAL//ACTUAL

New Customers
Commissions
New Team Members
Social Media Posts
Calls
Orders
New FB Friends
IG Following
Follow-Ups

Monday

Date   /   /

1 ....
2 ....
3 ....

TODAYS TOP GOALS

AFFIRMATIONS & GRATITUDE

TODAYS SCHEDULE

DAILY HABITS

☐
☐
☐
☐
☐
☐

SOCIAL MEDIA PLANNER

AM

12

PM

NOTES//IDEAS

TO-DO

☐
☐
☐
☐
☐
☐
☐
☐
☐
☐

Tuesday

Date   /   /

TODAYS TOP GOALS

1 . . . .
2 . . . .
3 . . . .

AFFIRMATIONS & GRATITUDE

TODAYS SCHEDULE

DAILY HABITS

SOCIAL MEDIA PLANNER

AM

12

PM

TO-DO

NOTES//IDEAS

Wednesday

1 ....
2 ....
3 ....

Date / /

AFFIRMATIONS & GRATITUDE

TODAYS SCHEDULE

DAILY HABITS

☐
☐
☐
☐
☐
☐

SOCIAL MEDIA PLANNER

AM

12

PM

TO-DO

☐
☐
☐
☐
☐
☐
☐
☐
☐

NOTES // IDEAS

Thursday

Date   /   /

TODAYS TOP GOALS

1 ....
2 ....
3 ....

AFFIRMATIONS & GRATITUDE

TODAYS SCHEDULE

DAILY HABITS

SOCIAL MEDIA PLANNER

AM

12

PM

NOTES//IDEAS

TO-DO

Friday

Date   /   /

1 ....

2 ....

3 ....

AFFIRMATIONS & GRATITUDE

TODAYS SCHEDULE

DAILY HABITS

- [ ]
- [ ]
- [ ]
- [ ]
- [ ]
- [ ]

SOCIAL MEDIA PLANNER

AM

12

PM

TO-DO

- [ ]
- [ ]
- [ ]
- [ ]
- [ ]
- [ ]
- [ ]
- [ ]
- [ ]

NOTES // IDEAS

Saturday

Date   /   /

TODAYS TOP GOALS

1 . . . .
2 . . . .
3 . . . .

AFFIRMATIONS & GRATITUDE

TODAYS SCHEDULE

DAILY HABITS

SOCIAL MEDIA PLANNER

AM

12

PM

TO-DO

NOTES // IDEAS

Sunday

Date / /

AFFIRMATIONS & GRATITUDE

TODAYS SCHEDULE

DAILY HABITS

SOCIAL MEDIA PLANNER

AM

12

PM

TO-DO

NOTES//IDEAS

Weekly Plan & Goals

Dates / / - / /

1 ....
2 ....
3 ....
4 ....
5 ....

MONDAY

TUESDAY

WEDNESDAY

THURSDAY

FRIDAY

WEEKEND

TO-DO'S

home

- [ ]
- [ ]
- [ ]
- [ ]
- [ ]

work

- [ ]
- [ ]
- [ ]
- [ ]
- [ ]

GOALS

GOAL//ACTUAL

New Customers
Commissions
New Team Members
Social Media Posts
Calls
Orders
New FB Friends
IG Following
Follow-Ups

Monday

Date   /   /

TODAYS TOP GOALS

1 ....
2 ....
3 ....

AFFIRMATIONS & GRATITUDE

TODAYS SCHEDULE

DAILY HABITS

☐
☐
☐
☐
☐
☐

SOCIAL MEDIA PLANNER

AM

12

PM

TO-DO

☐
☐
☐
☐
☐
☐
☐
☐
☐
☐

NOTES // IDEAS

Tuesday

Date   /   /

TODAYS TOP GOALS

1 ....
2 ....
3 ....

AFFIRMATIONS & GRATITUDE

TODAYS SCHEDULE

DAILY HABITS

- [ ]
- [ ]
- [ ]
- [ ]
- [ ]
- [ ]

SOCIAL MEDIA PLANNER

AM

12

PM

NOTES//IDEAS

TO-DO

- [ ]
- [ ]
- [ ]
- [ ]
- [ ]
- [ ]
- [ ]
- [ ]
- [ ]

Wednesday

Date   /   /

AFFIRMATIONS & GRATITUDE

TODAYS SCHEDULE

DAILY HABITS

SOCIAL MEDIA PLANNER

AM

12

PM

NOTES // IDEAS

TO-DO

Thursday

Date / /

TODAYS TOP GOALS

1 ....
2 ....
3 ....

AFFIRMATIONS & GRATITUDE

TODAYS SCHEDULE

DAILY HABITS

- ☐
- ☐
- ☐
- ☐
- ☐
- ☐

SOCIAL MEDIA PLANNER

AM

12

PM

NOTES//IDEAS

TO-DO

- ☐
- ☐
- ☐
- ☐
- ☐
- ☐
- ☐
- ☐
- ☐

Friday

Date   /   /

1 ....

2 ....

3 ....

AFFIRMATIONS & GRATITUDE

TODAYS SCHEDULE

DAILY HABITS

☐
☐
☐
☐
☐
☐

SOCIAL MEDIA PLANNER

AM

12

PM

NOTES // IDEAS

TO-DO

☐
☐
☐
☐
☐
☐
☐
☐
☐

Saturday

Date / /

TODAYS TOP GOALS

1 ....
2 ....
3 ....

AFFIRMATIONS & GRATITUDE

TODAYS SCHEDULE

DAILY HABITS

SOCIAL MEDIA PLANNER

AM

12

PM

NOTES // IDEAS

TO-DO

Sunday

Date / /

TODAYS TOP GOALS

1 ....

2 ....

3 ....

AFFIRMATIONS & GRATITUDE

TODAYS SCHEDULE

DAILY HABITS

☐
☐
☐
☐
☐
☐

SOCIAL MEDIA PLANNER

AM

12

PM

NOTES // IDEAS

TO-DO

☐
☐
☐
☐
☐
☐
☐
☐

HABIT TRACKER

HABIT

	1	2	3	4	5	6	7	8	9	10	11	12	13	14	15	16	17	18	19	20	21	22	23	24	25	26	27	28	29	30

WHY IT IS IMPORTANT TO ME TO CREATE THESE HABITS

HABIT TRACKER

HABIT	1	2	3	4	5	6	7	8	9	10	11	12	13	14	15	16	17	18	19	20	21	22	23	24	25	26	27	28	29	30
____																														
____																														
____																														
____																														
____																														
____																														
____																														
____																														
____																														

WHY IT IS IMPORTANT TO ME TO CREATE THESE HABITS

HABIT TRACKER

HABIT

	1	2	3	4	5	6	7	8	9	10	11	12	13	14	15	16	17	18	19	20	21	22	23	24	25	26	27	28	29	30
_____																														
_____																														
_____																														
_____																														
_____																														
_____																														
_____																														
_____																														
_____																														

WHY IT IS IMPORTANT TO ME TO CREATE THESE HABITS

HABIT TRACKER

HABIT

	1	2	3	4	5	6	7	8	9	10	11	12	13	14	15	16	17	18	19	20	21	22	23	24	25	26	27	28	29	30

WHY IT IS IMPORTANT TO ME TO CREATE THESE HABITS

RETAIL CUSTOMERS

NAME	ORDER DATE	FOLLOW-UP DATE	PRODUCT//NOTES

RETAIL CUSTOMERS

NAME	ORDER DATE	FOLLOW-UP DATE	PRODUCT//NOTES

RETAIL CUSTOMERS

NAME	ORDER DATE	FOLLOW-UP DATE	PRODUCT//NOTES

RETAIL CUSTOMERS

NAME	ORDER DATE	FOLLOW-UP DATE	PRODUCT//NOTES

RETAIL CUSTOMERS

NAME	ORDER DATE	FOLLOW-UP DATE	PRODUCT//NOTES

CUSTOMERS

NAME	ORDER DATE	FOLLOW-UP DATE	PRODUCT//NOTES

CUSTOMERS

NAME	ORDER DATE	FOLLOW-UP DATE	PRODUCT//NOTES

CUSTOMERS

NAME	ORDER DATE	FOLLOW-UP DATE	PRODUCT//NOTES

CUSTOMERS

NAME	ORDER DATE	FOLLOW-UP DATE	PRODUCT//NOTES

CUSTOMERS

NAME	ORDER DATE	FOLLOW-UP DATE	PRODUCT//NOTES

PREFERRED CUSTOMERS

NAME	ORDER DATE	FOLLOW-UP DATE	PRODUCT//NOTES

PREFERRED CUSTOMERS

NAME	ORDER DATE	FOLLOW-UP DATE	PRODUCT//NOTES

PREFERRED CUSTOMERS

NAME	ORDER DATE	FOLLOW-UP DATE	PRODUCT//NOTES

PREFERRED CUSTOMERS

NAME	ORDER DATE	FOLLOW-UP DATE	PRODUCT//NOTES

PREFERRED CUSTOMERS

NAME	ORDER DATE	FOLLOW-UP DATE	PRODUCT//NOTES

FOLLOW - UPS

NAME	DATE	FOLLOW-UP DATE	PRODUCT//NOTES

FOLLOW - UPS

NAME	DATE	FOLLOW-UP DATE	PRODUCT//NOTES

FOLLOW - UPS

NAME	DATE	FOLLOW-UP DATE	PRODUCT//NOTES

FOLLOW - UPS

NAME	DATE	FOLLOW-UP DATE	PRODUCT//NOTES

FOLLOW - UPS

NAME	DATE	FOLLOW-UP DATE	PRODUCT//NOTES

FOLLOW - UPS

NAME	DATE	FOLLOW-UP DATE	PRODUCT//NOTES

FOLLOW - UPS

NAME	DATE	FOLLOW-UP DATE	PRODUCT//NOTES

FOLLOW - UPS

NAME	DATE	FOLLOW-UP DATE	PRODUCT//NOTES

FOLLOW - UPS

NAME	DATE	FOLLOW-UP DATE	PRODUCT//NOTES

FOLLOW - UPS

NAME	DATE	FOLLOW-UP DATE	PRODUCT//NOTES

FOLLOW - UPS

NAME	DATE	FOLLOW-UP DATE	PRODUCT//NOTES

TEAM MEMBER PROFILE

Name _____ Email _____

Cell _____ Address _____

Spouse _____ Kids _____

Pets _____ Hobbies _____

Favorite Products _____

Strengths _____

_____

Weaknesses _____

_____

Goals _____

_____

Why _____

_____

CONVERSATION DATE: CURRENT RANK: RANK GOAL:

NOTES

Goals Before Next Convo _____

_____

_____

Follow - Up Date: /   /

CONVERSATION DATE: CURRENT RANK: RANK GOAL:

NOTES

Goals Before Next Convo _____

_____

_____

Follow - Up Date: /   /

CONVERSATION DATE: CURRENT RANK: RANK GOAL:

NOTES

Goals Before Next Convo _____

_____

_____

Follow - Up Date: /   /

CONVERSATION DATE: CURRENT RANK: RANK GOAL:

NOTES

Goals Before Next Convo _____

_____

_____

Follow - Up Date: /   /

TEAM MEMBER PROFILE

Name _____ Email _____

Cell _____ Address _____

Spouse _____ Kids _____

Pets _____ Hobbies _____

Favorite Products _____

Strengths _____

_____

Weaknesses _____

_____

Goals _____

_____

Why _____

_____

CONVERSATION DATE: CURRENT RANK: RANK GOAL:

NOTES	Goals Before Next Convo _____
	_____
	_____
	Follow - Up Date: / /

CONVERSATION DATE: CURRENT RANK: RANK GOAL:

NOTES	Goals Before Next Convo _____
	_____
	_____
	Follow - Up Date: / /

CONVERSATION DATE: CURRENT RANK: RANK GOAL:

NOTES	Goals Before Next Convo _____
	_____
	_____
	Follow - Up Date: / /

CONVERSATION DATE: CURRENT RANK: RANK GOAL:

NOTES	Goals Before Next Convo _____
	_____
	_____
	Follow - Up Date: / /

TEAM MEMBER PROFILE

Name _____ Email _____

Cell _____ Address _____

Spouse _____ Kids _____

Pets _____ Hobbies _____

Favorite Products _____

Strengths _____

_____

Weaknesses _____

_____

Goals _____

_____

Why _____

_____

CONVERSATION DATE: CURRENT RANK: RANK GOAL:

NOTES

Goals Before Next Convo _____

_____

_____

Follow - Up Date: /   /

CONVERSATION DATE: CURRENT RANK: RANK GOAL:

NOTES

Goals Before Next Convo _____

_____

_____

Follow - Up Date: /   /

CONVERSATION DATE: CURRENT RANK: RANK GOAL:

NOTES

Goals Before Next Convo _____

_____

_____

Follow - Up Date: /   /

CONVERSATION DATE: CURRENT RANK: RANK GOAL:

NOTES

Goals Before Next Convo _____

_____

_____

Follow - Up Date: /   /

TEAM MEMBER PROFILE

Name _____ Email _____

Cell _____ Address _____

Spouse _____ Kids _____

Pets _____ Hobbies _____

Favorite Products _____

Strengths _____

_____

Weaknesses _____

_____

Goals _____

_____

Why _____

_____

CONVERSATION DATE: CURRENT RANK: RANK GOAL:

NOTES

Goals Before Next Convo _____

_____

_____

Follow - Up Date: /   /

CONVERSATION DATE: CURRENT RANK: RANK GOAL:

NOTES

Goals Before Next Convo _____

_____

_____

Follow - Up Date: /   /

CONVERSATION DATE: CURRENT RANK: RANK GOAL:

NOTES

Goals Before Next Convo _____

_____

_____

Follow - Up Date: /   /

CONVERSATION DATE: CURRENT RANK: RANK GOAL:

NOTES

Goals Before Next Convo _____

_____

_____

Follow - Up Date: /   /

TEAM MEMBER PROFILE

Name _____ Email _____

Cell _____ Address _____

Spouse _____ Kids _____

Pets _____ Hobbies _____

Favorite Products _____

Strengths _____

_____

Weaknesses _____

_____

Goals _____

_____

Why _____

_____

CONVERSATION DATE: CURRENT RANK: RANK GOAL:

NOTES

Goals Before Next Convo _____

_____

_____

Follow - Up Date: /   /

CONVERSATION DATE: CURRENT RANK: RANK GOAL:

NOTES

Goals Before Next Convo _____

_____

_____

Follow - Up Date: /   /

CONVERSATION DATE: CURRENT RANK: RANK GOAL:

NOTES

Goals Before Next Convo _____

_____

_____

Follow - Up Date: /   /

CONVERSATION DATE: CURRENT RANK: RANK GOAL:

NOTES

Goals Before Next Convo _____

_____

_____

Follow - Up Date: /   /

TEAM MEMBER PROFILE

Name _____ Email _____

Cell _____ Address _____

Spouse _____ Kids _____

Pets _____ Hobbies _____

Favorite Products _____

Strengths _____

_____

Weaknesses _____

_____

Goals _____

_____

Why _____

_____

CURRENT RANK: RANK GOAL:

NOTES

Goals Before Next Convo _____

_____

_____

Follow - Up Date: /   /

CONVERSATION DATE: CURRENT RANK: RANK GOAL:

NOTES

Goals Before Next Convo _____

_____

_____

Follow - Up Date: /   /

CONVERSATION DATE: CURRENT RANK: RANK GOAL:

NOTES

Goals Before Next Convo _____

_____

_____

Follow - Up Date: /   /

CONVERSATION DATE: CURRENT RANK: RANK GOAL:

NOTES

Goals Before Next Convo _____

_____

_____

Follow - Up Date: /   /

TEAM MEMBER PROFILE

Name _____ Email _____

Cell _____ Address _____

Spouse _____ Kids _____

Pets _____ Hobbies _____

Favorite Products _____

Strengths _____

_____

Weaknesses _____

_____

Goals _____

_____

Why _____

_____

CONVERSATION DATE: CURRENT RANK: RANK GOAL:

NOTES

Goals Before Next Convo _____

_____

_____

Follow - Up Date: /   /

CONVERSATION DATE: CURRENT RANK: RANK GOAL:

NOTES

Goals Before Next Convo _____

_____

_____

Follow - Up Date: /   /

CONVERSATION DATE: CURRENT RANK: RANK GOAL:

NOTES

Goals Before Next Convo _____

_____

_____

Follow - Up Date: /   /

CONVERSATION DATE: CURRENT RANK: RANK GOAL:

NOTES

Goals Before Next Convo _____

_____

_____

Follow - Up Date: /   /

TEAM MEMBER PROFILE

Name _____ Email _____

Cell _____ Address _____

Spouse _____ Kids _____

Pets _____ Hobbies _____

Favorite Products _____

Strengths _____

_____

Weaknesses _____

_____

Goals _____

_____

Why _____

_____

CONVERSATION DATE: CURRENT RANK: RANK GOAL:

NOTES

Goals Before Next Convo _____

_____

_____

Follow - Up Date: /   /

CONVERSATION DATE: CURRENT RANK: RANK GOAL:

NOTES

Goals Before Next Convo _____

_____

_____

Follow - Up Date: /   /

CONVERSATION DATE: CURRENT RANK: RANK GOAL:

NOTES

Goals Before Next Convo _____

_____

_____

Follow - Up Date: /   /

CONVERSATION DATE: CURRENT RANK: RANK GOAL:

NOTES

Goals Before Next Convo _____

_____

_____

Follow - Up Date: /   /

TEAM MEMBER PROFILE

Name _____ Email _____

Cell _____ Address _____

Spouse _____ Kids _____

Pets _____ Hobbies _____

Favorite Products _____

Strengths _____

_____

Weaknesses _____

_____

Goals _____

_____

Why _____

_____

CONVERSATION DATE: CURRENT RANK: RANK GOAL:

NOTES

Goals Before Next Convo _____

_____

_____

Follow - Up Date: /   /

CONVERSATION DATE: CURRENT RANK: RANK GOAL:

NOTES

Goals Before Next Convo _____

_____

_____

Follow - Up Date: /   /

CONVERSATION DATE: CURRENT RANK: RANK GOAL:

NOTES

Goals Before Next Convo _____

_____

_____

Follow - Up Date: /   /

CONVERSATION DATE: CURRENT RANK: RANK GOAL:

NOTES

Goals Before Next Convo _____

_____

_____

Follow - Up Date: /   /

TEAM MEMBER PROFILE

Name _____ Email _____

Cell _____ Address _____

Spouse _____ Kids _____

Pets _____ Hobbies _____

Favorite Products _____

Strengths _____

_____

Weaknesses _____

_____

Goals _____

_____

Why _____

_____

CONVERSATION DATE: CURRENT RANK: RANK GOAL:

NOTES

Goals Before Next Convo _____

_____

_____

Follow - Up Date: /   /

CONVERSATION DATE: CURRENT RANK: RANK GOAL:

NOTES

Goals Before Next Convo _____

_____

_____

Follow - Up Date: /   /

CONVERSATION DATE: CURRENT RANK: RANK GOAL:

NOTES

Goals Before Next Convo _____

_____

_____

Follow - Up Date: /   /

CONVERSATION DATE: CURRENT RANK: RANK GOAL:

NOTES

Goals Before Next Convo _____

_____

_____

Follow - Up Date: /   /

TEAM MEMBER PROFILE

Name _____ Email _____

Cell _____ Address _____

Spouse _____ Kids _____

Pets _____ Hobbies _____

Favorite Products _____

Strengths _____

_____

Weaknesses _____

_____

Goals _____

_____

Why _____

_____

CONVERSATION DATE: CURRENT RANK: RANK GOAL:

NOTES

Goals Before Next Convo _____

_____

_____

Follow - Up Date: /   /

CONVERSATION DATE: CURRENT RANK: RANK GOAL:

NOTES

Goals Before Next Convo _____

_____

_____

Follow - Up Date: /   /

CONVERSATION DATE: CURRENT RANK: RANK GOAL:

NOTES

Goals Before Next Convo _____

_____

_____

Follow - Up Date: /   /

CONVERSATION DATE: CURRENT RANK: RANK GOAL:

NOTES

Goals Before Next Convo _____

_____

_____

Follow - Up Date: /   /

TEAM MEMBER PROFILE

Name _____ Email _____

Cell _____ Address _____

Spouse _____ Kids _____

Pets _____ Hobbies _____

Favorite Products _____

Strengths _____

_____

Weaknesses _____

_____

Goals _____

_____

Why _____

_____

CONVERSATION DATE: CURRENT RANK: RANK GOAL:

NOTES

Goals Before Next Convo _____

_____

_____

Follow - Up Date: /   /

CONVERSATION DATE: CURRENT RANK: RANK GOAL:

NOTES

Goals Before Next Convo _____

_____

_____

Follow - Up Date: /   /

CONVERSATION DATE: CURRENT RANK: RANK GOAL:

NOTES

Goals Before Next Convo _____

_____

_____

Follow - Up Date: /   /

CONVERSATION DATE: CURRENT RANK: RANK GOAL:

NOTES

Goals Before Next Convo _____

_____

_____

Follow - Up Date: /   /

TEAM MEMBER PROFILE

Name _____ Email _____

Cell _____ Address _____

Spouse _____ Kids _____

Pets _____ Hobbies _____

Favorite Products _____

Strengths _____

_____

Weaknesses _____

_____

Goals _____

_____

Why _____

_____

CONVERSATION DATE: CURRENT RANK: RANK GOAL:

NOTES

Goals Before Next Convo _____

_____

_____

Follow - Up Date: /   /

CONVERSATION DATE: CURRENT RANK: RANK GOAL:

NOTES

Goals Before Next Convo _____

_____

_____

Follow - Up Date: /   /

CONVERSATION DATE: CURRENT RANK: RANK GOAL:

NOTES

Goals Before Next Convo _____

_____

_____

Follow - Up Date: /   /

CONVERSATION DATE: CURRENT RANK: RANK GOAL:

NOTES

Goals Before Next Convo _____

_____

_____

Follow - Up Date: /   /

TEAM MEMBER PROFILE

Name _____ Email _____

Cell _____ Address _____

Spouse _____ Kids _____

Pets _____ Hobbies _____

Favorite Products _____

Strengths _____

_____

Weaknesses _____

_____

Goals _____

_____

Why _____

_____

CONVERSATION DATE: CURRENT RANK: RANK GOAL:

NOTES

Goals Before Next Convo _____

_____

_____

Follow - Up Date: /   /

CONVERSATION DATE: CURRENT RANK: RANK GOAL:

NOTES

Goals Before Next Convo _____

_____

_____

Follow - Up Date: /   /

CONVERSATION DATE: CURRENT RANK: RANK GOAL:

NOTES

Goals Before Next Convo _____

_____

_____

Follow - Up Date: /   /

CONVERSATION DATE: CURRENT RANK: RANK GOAL:

NOTES

Goals Before Next Convo _____

_____

_____

Follow - Up Date: /   /

TEAM MEMBER PROFILE

Name _____ Email _____

Cell _____ Address _____

Spouse _____ Kids _____

Pets _____ Hobbies _____

Favorite Products _____

Strengths _____

_____

Weaknesses _____

_____

Goals _____

_____

Why _____

_____

CONVERSATION DATE: CURRENT RANK: RANK GOAL:

NOTES	Goals Before Next Convo _____
	_____
	_____
	Follow - Up Date: / /

CONVERSATION DATE: CURRENT RANK: RANK GOAL:

NOTES	Goals Before Next Convo _____
	_____
	_____
	Follow - Up Date: / /

CONVERSATION DATE: CURRENT RANK: RANK GOAL:

NOTES	Goals Before Next Convo _____
	_____
	_____
	Follow - Up Date: / /

CONVERSATION DATE: CURRENT RANK: RANK GOAL:

NOTES	Goals Before Next Convo _____
	_____
	_____
	Follow - Up Date: / /

TEAM MEMBER PROFILE

Name _____ Email _____

Cell _____ Address _____

Spouse _____ Kids _____

Pets _____ Hobbies _____

Favorite Products _____

Strengths _____

_____

Weaknesses _____

_____

Goals _____

_____

Why _____

_____

CONVERSATION DATE: CURRENT RANK: RANK GOAL:

NOTES

Goals Before Next Convo _____

_____

_____

Follow - Up Date: /   /

CONVERSATION DATE: CURRENT RANK: RANK GOAL:

NOTES

Goals Before Next Convo _____

_____

_____

Follow - Up Date: /   /

CONVERSATION DATE: CURRENT RANK: RANK GOAL:

NOTES

Goals Before Next Convo _____

_____

_____

Follow - Up Date: /   /

CONVERSATION DATE: CURRENT RANK: RANK GOAL:

NOTES

Goals Before Next Convo _____

_____

_____

Follow - Up Date: /   /

TEAM MEMBER PROFILE

Name _____ Email _____

Cell _____ Address _____

Spouse _____ Kids _____

Pets _____ Hobbies _____

Favorite Products _____

Strengths _____

_____

Weaknesses _____

_____

Goals _____

_____

Why _____

_____

CONVERSATION DATE: CURRENT RANK: RANK GOAL:

NOTES

Goals Before Next Convo _____

_____

_____

Follow - Up Date: /   /

CONVERSATION DATE: CURRENT RANK: RANK GOAL:

NOTES

Goals Before Next Convo _____

_____

_____

Follow - Up Date: /   /

CONVERSATION DATE: CURRENT RANK: RANK GOAL:

NOTES

Goals Before Next Convo _____

_____

_____

Follow - Up Date: /   /

CONVERSATION DATE: CURRENT RANK: RANK GOAL:

NOTES

Goals Before Next Convo _____

_____

_____

Follow - Up Date: /   /

TEAM MEMBER PROFILE

Name _____ Email _____

Cell _____ Address _____

Spouse _____ Kids _____

Pets _____ Hobbies _____

Favorite Products _____

Strengths _____

_____

Weaknesses _____

_____

Goals _____

_____

Why _____

_____

CONVERSATION DATE: CURRENT RANK: RANK GOAL:

NOTES	Goals Before Next Convo _____
	_____
	_____
	Follow - Up Date: / /

CONVERSATION DATE: CURRENT RANK: RANK GOAL:

NOTES	Goals Before Next Convo _____
	_____
	_____
	Follow - Up Date: / /

CONVERSATION DATE: CURRENT RANK: RANK GOAL:

NOTES	Goals Before Next Convo _____
	_____
	_____
	Follow - Up Date: / /

CONVERSATION DATE: CURRENT RANK: RANK GOAL:

NOTES	Goals Before Next Convo _____
	_____
	_____
	Follow - Up Date: / /

TEAM MEMBER PROFILE

Name _____ Email _____

Cell _____ Address _____

Spouse _____ Kids _____

Pets _____ Hobbies _____

Favorite Products _____

Strengths _____

_____

Weaknesses _____

_____

Goals _____

_____

Why _____

_____

CONVERSATION DATE: CURRENT RANK: RANK GOAL:

NOTES

Goals Before Next Convo _____

_____

_____

Follow - Up Date: /   /

CONVERSATION DATE: CURRENT RANK: RANK GOAL:

NOTES

Goals Before Next Convo _____

_____

_____

Follow - Up Date: /   /

CONVERSATION DATE: CURRENT RANK: RANK GOAL:

NOTES

Goals Before Next Convo _____

_____

_____

Follow - Up Date: /   /

CONVERSATION DATE: CURRENT RANK: RANK GOAL:

NOTES

Goals Before Next Convo _____

_____

_____

Follow - Up Date: /   /

TEAM MEMBER PROFILE

Name _____ Email _____

Cell _____ Address _____

Spouse _____ Kids _____

Pets _____ Hobbies _____

Favorite Products _____

Strengths _____

_____

Weaknesses _____

_____

Goals _____

_____

Why _____

_____

CONVERSATION DATE: CURRENT RANK: RANK GOAL:

NOTES

Goals Before Next Convo _____

_____

_____

Follow - Up Date: /   /

CONVERSATION DATE: CURRENT RANK: RANK GOAL:

NOTES

Goals Before Next Convo _____

_____

_____

Follow - Up Date: /   /

CONVERSATION DATE: CURRENT RANK: RANK GOAL:

NOTES

Goals Before Next Convo _____

_____

_____

Follow - Up Date: /   /

CONVERSATION DATE: CURRENT RANK: RANK GOAL:

NOTES

Goals Before Next Convo _____

_____

_____

Follow - Up Date: /   /

TEAM MEMBER PROFILE

Name _____ Email _____

Cell _____ Address _____

Spouse _____ Kids _____

Pets _____ Hobbies _____

Favorite Products _____

Strengths _____

_____

Weaknesses _____

_____

Goals _____

_____

Why _____

_____

CONVERSATION DATE: CURRENT RANK: RANK GOAL:

NOTES

Goals Before Next Convo _____

_____

_____

Follow - Up Date: /   /

CONVERSATION DATE: CURRENT RANK: RANK GOAL:

NOTES

Goals Before Next Convo _____

_____

_____

Follow - Up Date: /   /

CONVERSATION DATE: CURRENT RANK: RANK GOAL:

NOTES

Goals Before Next Convo _____

_____

_____

Follow - Up Date: /   /

CONVERSATION DATE: CURRENT RANK: RANK GOAL:

NOTES

Goals Before Next Convo _____

_____

_____

Follow - Up Date: /   /

TEAM MEMBER PROFILE

Name _____ Email _____

Cell _____ Address _____

Spouse _____ Kids _____

Pets _____ Hobbies _____

Favorite Products _____

Strengths _____

_____

Weaknesses _____

_____

Goals _____

_____

Why _____

_____

CONVERSATION DATE: CURRENT RANK: RANK GOAL:

NOTES

Goals Before Next Convo _____

_____

_____

Follow - Up Date: /   /

CONVERSATION DATE: CURRENT RANK: RANK GOAL:

NOTES

Goals Before Next Convo _____

_____

_____

Follow - Up Date: /   /

CONVERSATION DATE: CURRENT RANK: RANK GOAL:

NOTES

Goals Before Next Convo _____

_____

_____

Follow - Up Date: /   /

CONVERSATION DATE: CURRENT RANK: RANK GOAL:

NOTES

Goals Before Next Convo _____

_____

_____

Follow - Up Date: /   /

TEAM MEMBER PROFILE

Name _____ Email _____

Cell _____ Address _____

Spouse _____ Kids _____

Pets _____ Hobbies _____

Favorite Products _____

Strengths _____

_____

Weaknesses _____

_____

Goals _____

_____

Why _____

_____

CONVERSATION DATE: CURRENT RANK: RANK GOAL:

NOTES

Goals Before Next Convo _____

_____

_____

Follow - Up Date: /   /

CONVERSATION DATE: CURRENT RANK: RANK GOAL:

NOTES

Goals Before Next Convo _____

_____

_____

Follow - Up Date: /   /

CONVERSATION DATE: CURRENT RANK: RANK GOAL:

NOTES

Goals Before Next Convo _____

_____

_____

Follow - Up Date: /   /

CONVERSATION DATE: CURRENT RANK: RANK GOAL:

NOTES

Goals Before Next Convo _____

_____

_____

Follow - Up Date: /   /

TEAM MEMBER PROFILE

Name _____ Email _____

Cell _____ Address _____

Spouse _____ Kids _____

Pets _____ Hobbies _____

Favorite Products _____

Strengths _____

_____

Weaknesses _____

_____

Goals _____

_____

Why _____

_____

CONVERSATION DATE: CURRENT RANK: RANK GOAL:

NOTES

Goals Before Next Convo _____

_____

_____

Follow - Up Date: /   /

CONVERSATION DATE: CURRENT RANK: RANK GOAL:

NOTES

Goals Before Next Convo _____

_____

_____

Follow - Up Date: /   /

CONVERSATION DATE: CURRENT RANK: RANK GOAL:

NOTES

Goals Before Next Convo _____

_____

_____

Follow - Up Date: /   /

CONVERSATION DATE: CURRENT RANK: RANK GOAL:

NOTES

Goals Before Next Convo _____

_____

_____

Follow - Up Date: /   /

TEAM MEMBER PROFILE

Name _____ Email _____

Cell _____ Address _____

Spouse _____ Kids _____

Pets _____ Hobbies _____

Favorite Products _____

Strengths _____

_____

Weaknesses _____

_____

Goals _____

_____

Why _____

_____

CONVERSATION DATE: CURRENT RANK: RANK GOAL:

NOTES

Goals Before Next Convo _____

_____

_____

Follow - Up Date: /   /

CONVERSATION DATE: CURRENT RANK: RANK GOAL:

NOTES

Goals Before Next Convo _____

_____

_____

Follow - Up Date: /   /

CONVERSATION DATE: CURRENT RANK: RANK GOAL:

NOTES

Goals Before Next Convo _____

_____

_____

Follow - Up Date: /   /

CONVERSATION DATE: CURRENT RANK: RANK GOAL:

NOTES

Goals Before Next Convo _____

_____

_____

Follow - Up Date: /   /

TEAM MEMBER PROFILE

Name _____ Email _____

Cell _____ Address _____

Spouse _____ Kids _____

Pets _____ Hobbies _____

Favorite Products _____

Strengths _____

_____

Weaknesses _____

_____

Goals _____

_____

Why _____

_____

CONVERSATION DATE: CURRENT RANK: RANK GOAL:

NOTES

Goals Before Next Convo _____

_____

_____

Follow - Up Date: /   /

CONVERSATION DATE: CURRENT RANK: RANK GOAL:

NOTES

Goals Before Next Convo _____

_____

_____

Follow - Up Date: /   /

CONVERSATION DATE: CURRENT RANK: RANK GOAL:

NOTES

Goals Before Next Convo _____

_____

_____

Follow - Up Date: /   /

CONVERSATION DATE: CURRENT RANK: RANK GOAL:

NOTES

Goals Before Next Convo _____

_____

_____

Follow - Up Date: /   /

TEAM MEMBER PROFILE

Name _____ Email _____

Cell _____ Address _____

Spouse _____ Kids _____

Pets _____ Hobbies _____

Favorite Products _____

Strengths _____

_____

Weaknesses _____

_____

Goals _____

_____

Why _____

_____

CONVERSATION DATE: CURRENT RANK: RANK GOAL:

NOTES

Goals Before Next Convo _____

_____

_____

Follow - Up Date: /   /

CONVERSATION DATE: CURRENT RANK: RANK GOAL:

NOTES

Goals Before Next Convo _____

_____

_____

Follow - Up Date: /   /

CONVERSATION DATE: CURRENT RANK: RANK GOAL:

NOTES

Goals Before Next Convo _____

_____

_____

Follow - Up Date: /   /

CONVERSATION DATE: CURRENT RANK: RANK GOAL:

NOTES

Goals Before Next Convo _____

_____

_____

Follow - Up Date: /   /

TEAM MEMBER PROFILE

Name _____ Email _____

Cell _____ Address _____

Spouse _____ Kids _____

Pets _____ Hobbies _____

Favorite Products _____

Strengths _____

_____

Weaknesses _____

_____

Goals _____

_____

Why _____

_____

CONVERSATION DATE: CURRENT RANK: RANK GOAL:

NOTES

Goals Before Next Convo _____

_____

_____

Follow - Up Date: /   /

CONVERSATION DATE: CURRENT RANK: RANK GOAL:

NOTES

Goals Before Next Convo _____

_____

_____

Follow - Up Date: /   /

CONVERSATION DATE: CURRENT RANK: RANK GOAL:

NOTES

Goals Before Next Convo _____

_____

_____

Follow - Up Date: /   /

CONVERSATION DATE: CURRENT RANK: RANK GOAL:

NOTES

Goals Before Next Convo _____

_____

_____

Follow - Up Date: /   /

TEAM MEMBER PROFILE

Name _____ Email _____

Cell _____ Address _____

Spouse _____ Kids _____

Pets _____ Hobbies _____

Favorite Products _____

Strengths _____

_____

Weaknesses _____

_____

Goals _____

_____

Why _____

_____

CONVERSATION DATE: CURRENT RANK: RANK GOAL:

NOTES

Goals Before Next Convo _____

_____

_____

Follow - Up Date: /   /

CONVERSATION DATE: CURRENT RANK: RANK GOAL:

NOTES

Goals Before Next Convo _____

_____

_____

Follow - Up Date: /   /

CONVERSATION DATE: CURRENT RANK: RANK GOAL:

NOTES

Goals Before Next Convo _____

_____

_____

Follow - Up Date: /   /

CONVERSATION DATE: CURRENT RANK: RANK GOAL:

NOTES

Goals Before Next Convo _____

_____

_____

Follow - Up Date: /   /

TEAM MEMBER PROFILE

Name _____ Email _____

Cell _____ Address _____

Spouse _____ Kids _____

Pets _____ Hobbies _____

Favorite Products _____

Strengths _____

_____

Weaknesses _____

_____

Goals _____

_____

Why _____

_____

CONVERSATION DATE: CURRENT RANK: RANK GOAL:

NOTES

Goals Before Next Convo _____

_____

_____

Follow - Up Date: /   /

CONVERSATION DATE: CURRENT RANK: RANK GOAL:

NOTES

Goals Before Next Convo _____

_____

_____

Follow - Up Date: /   /

CONVERSATION DATE: CURRENT RANK: RANK GOAL:

NOTES

Goals Before Next Convo _____

_____

_____

Follow - Up Date: /   /

CONVERSATION DATE: CURRENT RANK: RANK GOAL:

NOTES

Goals Before Next Convo _____

_____

_____

Follow - Up Date: /   /

TEAM MEMBER PROFILE

Name _____ Email _____

Cell _____ Address _____

Spouse _____ Kids _____

Pets _____ Hobbies _____

Favorite Products _____

Strengths _____

_____

Weaknesses _____

_____

Goals _____

_____

Why _____

_____

CONVERSATION DATE: CURRENT RANK: RANK GOAL:

NOTES

Goals Before Next Convo _____

_____

_____

Follow - Up Date: /   /

CONVERSATION DATE: CURRENT RANK: RANK GOAL:

NOTES

Goals Before Next Convo _____

_____

_____

Follow - Up Date: /   /

CONVERSATION DATE: CURRENT RANK: RANK GOAL:

NOTES

Goals Before Next Convo _____

_____

_____

Follow - Up Date: /   /

CONVERSATION DATE: CURRENT RANK: RANK GOAL:

NOTES

Goals Before Next Convo _____

_____

_____

Follow - Up Date: /   /

TEAM MEMBER PROFILE

Name _____ Email _____

Cell _____ Address _____

Spouse _____ Kids _____

Pets _____ Hobbies _____

Favorite Products _____

Strengths _____

_____

Weaknesses _____

_____

Goals _____

_____

Why _____

_____

CONVERSATION DATE: CURRENT RANK: RANK GOAL:

NOTES

Goals Before Next Convo _____

_____

_____

Follow - Up Date: /   /

CONVERSATION DATE: CURRENT RANK: RANK GOAL:

NOTES

Goals Before Next Convo _____

_____

_____

Follow - Up Date: /   /

CONVERSATION DATE: CURRENT RANK: RANK GOAL:

NOTES

Goals Before Next Convo _____

_____

_____

Follow - Up Date: /   /

CONVERSATION DATE: CURRENT RANK: RANK GOAL:

NOTES

Goals Before Next Convo _____

_____

_____

Follow - Up Date: /   /

TEAM MEMBER PROFILE

Name _____ Email _____

Cell _____ Address _____

Spouse _____ Kids _____

Pets _____ Hobbies _____

Favorite Products _____

Strengths _____

_____

Weaknesses _____

_____

Goals _____

_____

Why _____

_____

CONVERSATION DATE: CURRENT RANK: RANK GOAL:

NOTES

Goals Before Next Convo _____

_____

_____

Follow - Up Date: /   /

CONVERSATION DATE: CURRENT RANK: RANK GOAL:

NOTES

Goals Before Next Convo _____

_____

_____

Follow - Up Date: /   /

CONVERSATION DATE: CURRENT RANK: RANK GOAL:

NOTES

Goals Before Next Convo _____

_____

_____

Follow - Up Date: /   /

CONVERSATION DATE: CURRENT RANK: RANK GOAL:

NOTES

Goals Before Next Convo _____

_____

_____

Follow - Up Date: /   /

TEAM MEMBER PROFILE

Name _____ Email _____

Cell _____ Address _____

Spouse _____ Kids _____

Pets _____ Hobbies _____

Favorite Products _____

Strengths _____

_____

Weaknesses _____

_____

Goals _____

_____

Why _____

_____

CONVERSATION DATE: CURRENT RANK: RANK GOAL:

NOTES

Goals Before Next Convo _____

_____

_____

Follow - Up Date: /   /

CONVERSATION DATE: CURRENT RANK: RANK GOAL:

NOTES

Goals Before Next Convo _____

_____

_____

Follow - Up Date: /   /

CONVERSATION DATE: CURRENT RANK: RANK GOAL:

NOTES

Goals Before Next Convo _____

_____

_____

Follow - Up Date: /   /

CONVERSATION DATE: CURRENT RANK: RANK GOAL:

NOTES

Goals Before Next Convo _____

_____

_____

Follow - Up Date: /   /

TEAM MEMBER PROFILE

Name _____ Email _____

Cell _____ Address _____

Spouse _____ Kids _____

Pets _____ Hobbies _____

Favorite Products _____

Strengths _____

_____

Weaknesses _____

_____

Goals _____

_____

Why _____

_____

CONVERSATION DATE: CURRENT RANK: RANK GOAL:

NOTES

Goals Before Next Convo _____

_____

_____

Follow - Up Date: /   /

CONVERSATION DATE: CURRENT RANK: RANK GOAL:

NOTES

Goals Before Next Convo _____

_____

_____

Follow - Up Date: /   /

CONVERSATION DATE: CURRENT RANK: RANK GOAL:

NOTES

Goals Before Next Convo _____

_____

_____

Follow - Up Date: /   /

CONVERSATION DATE: CURRENT RANK: RANK GOAL:

NOTES

Goals Before Next Convo _____

_____

_____

Follow - Up Date: /   /

TEAM MEMBER PROFILE

Name _____ Email _____

Cell _____ Address _____

Spouse _____ Kids _____

Pets _____ Hobbies _____

Favorite Products _____

Strengths _____

_____

Weaknesses _____

_____

Goals _____

_____

Why _____

_____

CONVERSATION DATE: CURRENT RANK: RANK GOAL:

NOTES	Goals Before Next Convo _____
	_____
	_____
	Follow - Up Date: / /

CONVERSATION DATE: CURRENT RANK: RANK GOAL:

NOTES	Goals Before Next Convo _____
	_____
	_____
	Follow - Up Date: / /

CONVERSATION DATE: CURRENT RANK: RANK GOAL:

NOTES	Goals Before Next Convo _____
	_____
	_____
	Follow - Up Date: / /

CONVERSATION DATE: CURRENT RANK: RANK GOAL:

NOTES	Goals Before Next Convo _____
	_____
	_____
	Follow - Up Date: / /

TEAM MEMBER PROFILE

Name _____ Email _____

Cell _____ Address _____

Spouse _____ Kids _____

Pets _____ Hobbies _____

Favorite Products _____

Strengths _____

_____

Weaknesses _____

_____

Goals _____

_____

Why _____

_____

CONVERSATION DATE: CURRENT RANK: RANK GOAL:

NOTES

Goals Before Next Convo _____

_____

_____

Follow - Up Date: /   /

CONVERSATION DATE: CURRENT RANK: RANK GOAL:

NOTES

Goals Before Next Convo _____

_____

_____

Follow - Up Date: /   /

CONVERSATION DATE: CURRENT RANK: RANK GOAL:

NOTES

Goals Before Next Convo _____

_____

_____

Follow - Up Date: /   /

CONVERSATION DATE: CURRENT RANK: RANK GOAL:

NOTES

Goals Before Next Convo _____

_____

_____

Follow - Up Date: /   /

TEAM MEMBER PROFILE

Name _____ Email _____

Cell _____ Address _____

Spouse _____ Kids _____

Pets _____ Hobbies _____

Favorite Products _____

Strengths _____

_____

Weaknesses _____

_____

Goals _____

_____

Why _____

_____

CONVERSATION DATE: CURRENT RANK: RANK GOAL:

NOTES

Goals Before Next Convo _____

_____

_____

Follow - Up Date: /   /

CONVERSATION DATE: CURRENT RANK: RANK GOAL:

NOTES

Goals Before Next Convo _____

_____

_____

Follow - Up Date: /   /

CONVERSATION DATE: CURRENT RANK: RANK GOAL:

NOTES

Goals Before Next Convo _____

_____

_____

Follow - Up Date: /   /

CONVERSATION DATE: CURRENT RANK: RANK GOAL:

NOTES

Goals Before Next Convo _____

_____

_____

Follow - Up Date: /   /

TEAM MEMBER PROFILE

Name _____ Email _____

Cell _____ Address _____

Spouse _____ Kids _____

Pets _____ Hobbies _____

Favorite Products _____

Strengths _____

_____

Weaknesses _____

_____

Goals _____

_____

Why _____

_____

CONVERSATION DATE: CURRENT RANK: RANK GOAL:

NOTES

Goals Before Next Convo _____

_____

_____

Follow - Up Date: /   /

CONVERSATION DATE: CURRENT RANK: RANK GOAL:

NOTES

Goals Before Next Convo _____

_____

_____

Follow - Up Date: /   /

CONVERSATION DATE: CURRENT RANK: RANK GOAL:

NOTES

Goals Before Next Convo _____

_____

_____

Follow - Up Date: /   /

CONVERSATION DATE: CURRENT RANK: RANK GOAL:

NOTES

Goals Before Next Convo _____

_____

_____

Follow - Up Date: /   /

TEAM MEMBER PROFILE

Name _____ Email _____

Cell _____ Address _____

Spouse _____ Kids _____

Pets _____ Hobbies _____

Favorite Products _____

Strengths _____

_____

Weaknesses _____

_____

Goals _____

_____

Why _____

_____

CONVERSATION DATE: CURRENT RANK: RANK GOAL:

NOTES

Goals Before Next Convo _____

_____

_____

Follow - Up Date: /   /

CONVERSATION DATE: CURRENT RANK: RANK GOAL:

NOTES

Goals Before Next Convo _____

_____

_____

Follow - Up Date: /   /

CONVERSATION DATE: CURRENT RANK: RANK GOAL:

NOTES

Goals Before Next Convo _____

_____

_____

Follow - Up Date: /   /

CONVERSATION DATE: CURRENT RANK: RANK GOAL:

NOTES

Goals Before Next Convo _____

_____

_____

Follow - Up Date: /   /

ONLINE EVENT PLANNER

Host _____
Start Date _____
End Date _____
Event Name _____

Host _____
Start Date _____
End Date _____
Event Name _____

POST DATES	POST DATES

S	M	T	W	T	F	S		S	M	T	W	T	F	S
☐	☐	☐	☐	☐	☐	☐		☐	☐	☐	☐	☐	☐	☐

NOTES//IDEAS

NOTES//IDEAS

PARTICIPANTS	ORDERS	PARTICIPANTS	ORDERS

ONLINE EVENT PLANNER

Host _____	Host _____
Start Date _____	Start Date _____
End Date _____	End Date _____
Event Name _____	Event Name _____

POST DATES	POST DATES
S M T W T F S	S M T W T F S
☐ ☐ ☐ ☐ ☐ ☐ ☐	☐ ☐ ☐ ☐ ☐ ☐ ☐

NOTES//IDEAS	NOTES//IDEAS

PARTICIPANTS	ORDERS	PARTICIPANTS	ORDERS
_____	____	_____	____
_____	____	_____	____
_____	____	_____	____
_____	____	_____	____
_____	____	_____	____
_____	____	_____	____
_____	____	_____	____
_____	____	_____	____
_____	____	_____	____
_____	____	_____	____
_____	____	_____	____
_____	____	_____	____
_____	____	_____	____
_____	____	_____	____
_____	____	_____	____
_____	____	_____	____
_____	____	_____	____
_____	____	_____	____
_____	____	_____	____
_____	____	_____	____
_____	____	_____	____
_____	____	_____	____

ONLINE EVENT PLANNER

Host _____

Start Date _____

End Date _____

Event Name _____

Host _____

Start Date _____

End Date _____

Event Name _____

POST DATES	POST DATES

S	M	T	W	T	F	S
☐	☐	☐	☐	☐	☐	☐

S	M	T	W	T	F	S
☐	☐	☐	☐	☐	☐	☐

NOTES//IDEAS

NOTES//IDEAS

PARTICIPANTS	ORDERS	PARTICIPANTS	ORDERS

ONLINE EVENT PLANNER

Host _____

Start Date _____

End Date _____

Event Name _____

Host _____

Start Date _____

End Date _____

Event Name _____

POST DATES

S	M	T	W	T	F	S
☐	☐	☐	☐	☐	☐	☐

POST DATES

S	M	T	W	T	F	S
☐	☐	☐	☐	☐	☐	☐

NOTES//IDEAS

NOTES//IDEAS

PARTICIPANTS	ORDERS	PARTICIPANTS	ORDERS

ONLINE EVENT PLANNER

Host _____	Host _____
Start Date _____	Start Date _____
End Date _____	End Date _____
Event Name _____	Event Name _____

POST DATES	POST DATES

S	M	T	W	T	F	S		S	M	T	W	T	F	S
☐	☐	☐	☐	☐	☐	☐		☐	☐	☐	☐	☐	☐	☐

NOTES//IDEAS	NOTES//IDEAS

PARTICIPANTS	ORDERS	PARTICIPANTS	ORDERS
_____	_____	_____	_____
_____	_____	_____	_____
_____	_____	_____	_____
_____	_____	_____	_____
_____	_____	_____	_____
_____	_____	_____	_____
_____	_____	_____	_____
_____	_____	_____	_____
_____	_____	_____	_____
_____	_____	_____	_____
_____	_____	_____	_____
_____	_____	_____	_____
_____	_____	_____	_____
_____	_____	_____	_____
_____	_____	_____	_____
_____	_____	_____	_____
_____	_____	_____	_____
_____	_____	_____	_____
_____	_____	_____	_____
_____	_____	_____	_____
_____	_____	_____	_____
_____	_____	_____	_____
_____	_____	_____	_____

ONLINE EVENT PLANNER

Host _____

Start Date _____

End Date _____

Event Name _____

Host _____

Start Date _____

End Date _____

Event Name _____

POST DATES

S	M	T	W	T	F	S
☐	☐	☐	☐	☐	☐	☐

NOTES//IDEAS

POST DATES

S	M	T	W	T	F	S
☐	☐	☐	☐	☐	☐	☐

NOTES//IDEAS

PARTICIPANTS	ORDERS
_____	_____
_____	_____
_____	_____
_____	_____
_____	_____
_____	_____
_____	_____
_____	_____
_____	_____
_____	_____
_____	_____
_____	_____
_____	_____
_____	_____
_____	_____
_____	_____
_____	_____
_____	_____
_____	_____
_____	_____
_____	_____
_____	_____

PARTICIPANTS	ORDERS
_____	_____
_____	_____
_____	_____
_____	_____
_____	_____
_____	_____
_____	_____
_____	_____
_____	_____
_____	_____
_____	_____
_____	_____
_____	_____
_____	_____
_____	_____
_____	_____
_____	_____
_____	_____
_____	_____
_____	_____
_____	_____
_____	_____

ONLINE EVENT PLANNER

Host _____
Start Date _____
End Date _____
Event Name _____

Host _____
Start Date _____
End Date _____
Event Name _____

POST DATES

S	M	T	W	T	F	S
□	□	□	□	□	□	□

POST DATES

S	M	T	W	T	F	S
□	□	□	□	□	□	□

NOTES//IDEAS

NOTES//IDEAS

PARTICIPANTS	ORDERS

PARTICIPANTS	ORDERS

ONLINE EVENT PLANNER

Host _____   Host _____
Start Date _____   Start Date _____
End Date _____   End Date _____
Event Name _____   Event Name _____

POST DATES							POST DATES					
S	M	T	W	T	F	S	S	M	T	W	T	F	S
☐	☐	☐	☐	☐	☐	☐	☐	☐	☐	☐	☐	☐	☐

NOTES//IDEAS   NOTES//IDEAS

PARTICIPANTS	ORDERS	PARTICIPANTS	ORDERS
_____	_____	_____	_____
_____	_____	_____	_____
_____	_____	_____	_____
_____	_____	_____	_____
_____	_____	_____	_____
_____	_____	_____	_____
_____	_____	_____	_____
_____	_____	_____	_____
_____	_____	_____	_____
_____	_____	_____	_____
_____	_____	_____	_____
_____	_____	_____	_____
_____	_____	_____	_____
_____	_____	_____	_____
_____	_____	_____	_____
_____	_____	_____	_____
_____	_____	_____	_____
_____	_____	_____	_____
_____	_____	_____	_____
_____	_____	_____	_____
_____	_____	_____	_____
_____	_____	_____	_____
_____	_____	_____	_____
_____	_____	_____	_____
_____	_____	_____	_____
_____	_____	_____	_____

ONLINE EVENT PLANNER

Host _____
Start Date _____
End Date _____
Event Name _____

Host _____
Start Date _____
End Date _____
Event Name _____

POST DATES

S	M	T	W	T	F	S
☐	☐	☐	☐	☐	☐	☐

POST DATES

S	M	T	W	T	F	S
☐	☐	☐	☐	☐	☐	☐

NOTES//IDEAS

NOTES//IDEAS

PARTICIPANTS	ORDERS

PARTICIPANTS	ORDERS

ONLINE EVENT PLANNER

Host _____
Start Date _____
End Date _____
Event Name _____

Host _____
Start Date _____
End Date _____
Event Name _____

POST DATES

S	M	T	W	T	F	S
☐	☐	☐	☐	☐	☐	☐

NOTES//IDEAS

POST DATES

S	M	T	W	T	F	S
☐	☐	☐	☐	☐	☐	☐

NOTES//IDEAS

PARTICIPANTS	ORDERS	PARTICIPANTS	ORDERS

ONLINE EVENT PLANNER

Host _____	Host _____
Start Date _____	Start Date _____
End Date _____	End Date _____
Event Name _____	Event Name _____

POST DATES	POST DATES
S M T W T F S	S M T W T F S
☐ ☐ ☐ ☐ ☐ ☐ ☐	☐ ☐ ☐ ☐ ☐ ☐ ☐

NOTES//IDEAS	NOTES//IDEAS

PARTICIPANTS	ORDERS	PARTICIPANTS	ORDERS
_____	_____	_____	_____
_____	_____	_____	_____
_____	_____	_____	_____
_____	_____	_____	_____
_____	_____	_____	_____
_____	_____	_____	_____
_____	_____	_____	_____
_____	_____	_____	_____
_____	_____	_____	_____
_____	_____	_____	_____
_____	_____	_____	_____
_____	_____	_____	_____
_____	_____	_____	_____
_____	_____	_____	_____
_____	_____	_____	_____
_____	_____	_____	_____
_____	_____	_____	_____
_____	_____	_____	_____
_____	_____	_____	_____
_____	_____	_____	_____
_____	_____	_____	_____
_____	_____	_____	_____

ONLINE EVENT PLANNER

Host _____	Host _____
Start Date _____	Start Date _____
End Date _____	End Date _____
Event Name _____	Event Name _____

POST DATES	POST DATES
S M T W T F S	S M T W T F S
☐ ☐ ☐ ☐ ☐ ☐ ☐	☐ ☐ ☐ ☐ ☐ ☐ ☐

NOTES//IDEAS	NOTES//IDEAS

PARTICIPANTS	ORDERS	PARTICIPANTS	ORDERS
_____	_____	_____	_____
_____	_____	_____	_____
_____	_____	_____	_____
_____	_____	_____	_____
_____	_____	_____	_____
_____	_____	_____	_____
_____	_____	_____	_____
_____	_____	_____	_____
_____	_____	_____	_____
_____	_____	_____	_____
_____	_____	_____	_____
_____	_____	_____	_____
_____	_____	_____	_____
_____	_____	_____	_____
_____	_____	_____	_____
_____	_____	_____	_____
_____	_____	_____	_____
_____	_____	_____	_____
_____	_____	_____	_____
_____	_____	_____	_____
_____	_____	_____	_____
_____	_____	_____	_____
_____	_____	_____	_____

TEAM CALL NOTES

Date   /   /

SPEAKER: **TOPIC:**

TEAM CALL NOTES

Date   /   /

SPEAKER: TOPIC:

TEAM CALL NOTES

Date   /   /

SPEAKER: **TOPIC:**

TEAM CALL NOTES

Date   /   /

SPEAKER: **TOPIC:**

TEAM CALL NOTES

Date   /   /

TEAM CALL NOTES

Date / /

SPEAKER: TOPIC:

TEAM CALL NOTES

Date   /   /

SPEAKER: TOPIC:

TEAM CALL NOTES

Date   /   /

SPEAKER: **TOPIC:**

TEAM CALL NOTES

Date   /   /

SPEAKER: **TOPIC:**

TEAM CALL NOTES

Date   /   /

SPEAKER: **TOPIC:**

TEAM CALL NOTES

Date   /   /

TEAM CALL NOTES

Date   /   /

SPEAKER: **TOPIC:**

TEAM CALL NOTES

Date / /

TEAM CALL NOTES

Date   /   /

SPEAKER: **TOPIC:**

TEAM CALL NOTES

Date   /   /

TEAM CALL NOTES

Date   /   /

SPEAKER: **TOPIC:**

NOTES & BRILLIANT IDEAS

NOTES & BRILLIANT IDEAS

NOTES & BRILLIANT IDEAS

NOTES & BRILLIANT IDEAS

NOTES & BRILLIANT IDEAS

NOTES & BRILLIANT IDEAS

NOTES & BRILLIANT IDEAS

NOTES & BRILLIANT IDEAS

Made in United States
North Haven, CT
03 January 2023

30476895R00122